DINOSAUR
INFOSAURUS

KILLER DINOSAURS

Katie Woolley

WAYLAND

www.waylandbooks.co.uk

First published in Great Britain in 2017
by Wayland

Copyright © Hodder and Stoughton 2017

Editor: Elise Short
Design: Peter Clayman
Illustrations: Martin Bustamante

ISBN: 978 1 5263 0461 2

10 9 8 7 6 5 4 3 2 1

Wayland, an imprint of
Hachette Children's Group
Part of Hodder and Stoughton
Carmelite House
50 Victoria Embankment
London EC4Y 0DZ

An Hachette UK Company
www.hachette.co.uk
www.hachettechildrens.co.uk

Printed and bound in China

Picture acknowledgements:
All images courtesy of Shutterstock except
cover image; p11 ;p23; p25; p27: illustrations by
Martin Bustamante

CONTENTS

DEADLY HUNTERS

Meat-eating dinosaurs – the **carnivores** – were killing machines! Most were theropods that came in all shapes and sizes, from enormous beasts, such as **Tyrannosaurus rex** and **Allosaurus**, to teeny-tiny dinosaurs like **Microraptor**.

This mighty meat-eater is Tyrannosaurus rex, pronounced **tie-RAN-oh-sore-us rex**, its name means tyrant lizard king.

Hesperonychus [hes-puh-ruh-NIE-kuss] was a **tiny** meat-eater that weighed no more than a **chicken**!

Many meat-eaters walked on two feet. This made them **fast** and meant they could catch their prey with their clawed hands.

This feathery creature is **Microraptor**, pronounced **MIKE-row-rap-tor**. Its name means tiny thief.

Microraptor had long flight feathers on all four limbs. These may have allowed it to **glide** between trees in search of **prey**, such as insects.

Killer dinosaurs used their good sense of **smell** and excellent **eyesight** to find their food!

Allosaurus
[AL-oh-saw-russ]

Most meat-eaters had very short, strong front arms. Albertonykus [al-BERT-oh-NIE-kuss] used its **talons** to **dig into** rotten wood where **termites** lived.

All dinosaurs had **small brains** for their bodies, but meat-eaters were said to be the smartest. **Troodon** [TROH-oh-don] might have been the most intelligent. It was 2 m long and had a brain the same size as an ostrich's brain.

brain

5

BUILT TO KILL

Meat-eating dinosaurs had to **hunt** or **scavenge** to stay alive. They were **made for speed** with strong hind legs to chase down their prey.

Many killer dinosaurs had long **tails**, which they held horizontally, to **balance** out their strong necks, big heads and powerful jaws.

Scientists don't know for sure, but a meat-eater's **skin** or **feathers** probably helped it **blend in** with its surroundings when on the hunt for food.

Some meat-eaters may have been **nocturnal hunters**. Troodon had big, cat-like **eyes** that could seek out prey in the darkness.

6

Like **sharks** and **crocodiles**, most meat-eating dinosaurs would **grow** a new **tooth** to replace any that fell out or broke.

Tyrannosaurus rex had over 50 teeth! Each one was **23 cm long** - that's as long as a **banana**!

Killer dinosaurs had powerful jaws that snapped shut like a **crocodile**. They also had **sharp teeth** that could cut through flesh and bone.

Some palaeontologists think that even though T. rex had **short arms** it might still have been able to grasp **up to 180 kg** of prey. That's like being able to hold on to a **gorilla**!

This beast is **Saurophaganax**, pronounced **sore-oh-fag-ah-naks**. Its name means king of the lizard eaters.

DINOSAUR DINNERS

All dinosaurs were part of a **food chain**. There were lots of **plants** to feed the **plant-eaters** at the bottom of the food chain. These plant-eaters were then gobbled up by the **meat-eaters**.

Some meat-eating dinosaurs may have also been **scavengers**. A scavenger is an animal that finds and eats the **carcass** of other dinosaurs, rather than hunting for its next meal.

Not all meat-eating dinosaurs hunted other dinosaurs. **Some of them ate fish, insects, eggs and mammals.** The teeth of some dinosaurs, such as Gallimimus [gal-lee-MEEM-us], were adapted to eat both meat and plants.

8

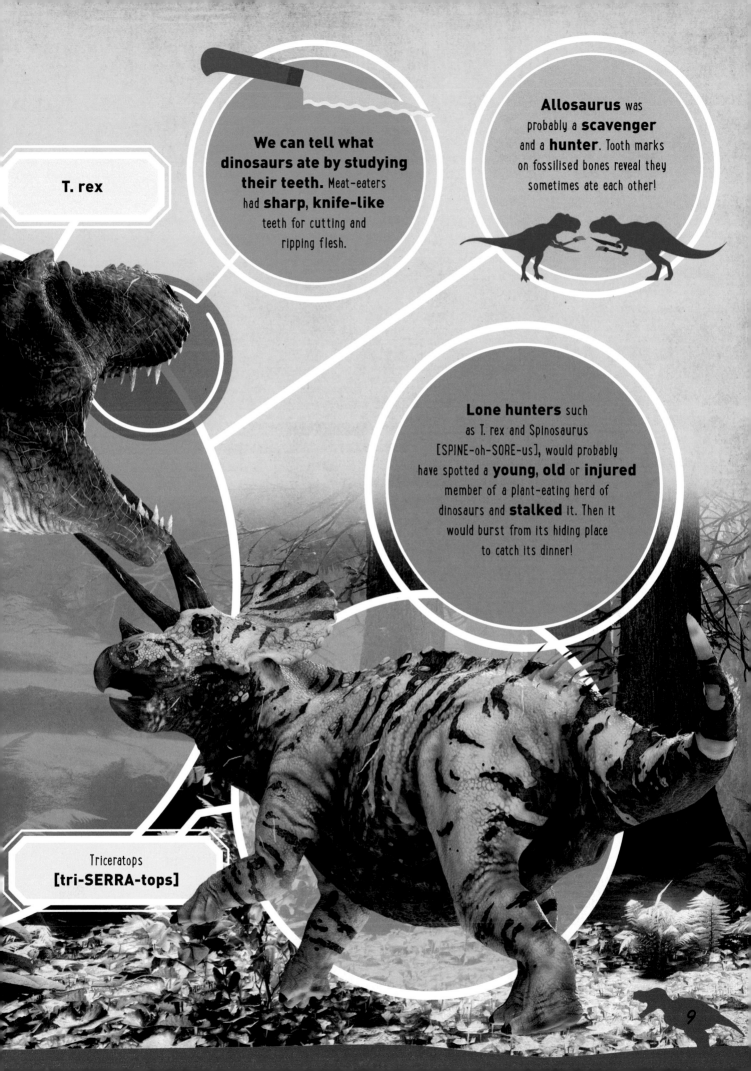

T. rex

We can tell what dinosaurs ate by studying their teeth. Meat-eaters had **sharp, knife-like** teeth for cutting and ripping flesh.

Allosaurus was probably a **scavenger** and a **hunter**. Tooth marks on fossilised bones reveal they sometimes ate each other!

Lone hunters such as T. rex and Spinosaurus [SPINE-oh-SORE-us], would probably have spotted a **young, old** or **injured** member of a plant-eating herd of dinosaurs and **stalked** it. Then it would burst from its hiding place to catch its dinner!

Triceratops
[tri-SERRA-tops]

9

DINO GANGS

Scientists also think some meat-eaters **hunted in packs**, like wolves and hyenas do today. They used their intelligence to **work together** and catch prey that was much bigger than them.

Tenontosaurus

Deinonychus [die-NON-i-kuss] is one dinosaur that probably hunted in groups. It may have **attacked** prey much larger than itself, like **Tenontosaurus** [ten-ON-toe-sore-us]. The group might have held down their prey with their strong legs and claws, and possibly even started eating it while it was still alive!

Eoraptor [EE-oh-RAP-tor] **was one of the earliest pack-hunting dinosaurs.** It had **eyes** on the side of its head for **all-round vision**.

The pack-hunting **Megaraptor** [meg-a-RAP-tor] was a meat-eating theropod. Each one weighed as much as a **black rhino** and could possibly run as fast as an **ostrich**. Imagine a pack charging towards you!

Utahraptor, pronounced **YOO-tah-RAP-tor**, means Utah thief.

Pronounced **ig-WHA-noh-don**, Iguanodon's name means Iguana tooth.

In 2014, a huge block of sandstone was pulled from a mountain in Utah, USA. It has been nicknamed the '**death trap**' as six or more meat-eating **Utahraptors** have been found there. Did they die together **hunting as a pack**?

The discovery of 22 individual **Albertosaurus** [al-BERT-oh-saw-russ] fossils found together suggests that these dinosaurs hunted in packs. The bones were a mix of young and adult Albertosaurus. Some scientists think it's even possible that the younger, faster Albertosaurus **drove prey** towards the jaws of the stronger adult dinosaurs.

11

TERRIFYING T. REX

Tyrannosaurus rex was one of the **strongest** and **biggest** of the deadly dinosaurs. It lived throughout what is now North America during the last part of the **Cretaceous period.**

T. rex could grow to 12 m in length and 4 m tall. That's more than the length of a double-decker bus but the same height.

New scientific methods have helped scientists to **discover** that T. rex probably had tough, scraggly **feathers** on parts of its body.

It could weigh up to 7,000 kg. That's the same weight as **two hippos.**

In one bite, **T. rex could fit 225 kg of meat in its mouth.** That's the equivalent of **two-and-a-half sheep** per mouthful!

A T. rex **eyeball** was the same size as a human adult's fist!

The **force** of its **bite** would have felt like the weight of **five small cars** crashing down on whatever it was crunching! This makes the T. rex the **hardest-biting** land animal ever known.

T. rex liked to **hunt** large **plant-eaters**, but it was also a **scavenger**, eating already-dead animals.

SCARY SPINOSAURUS

Spinosaurus was the **largest** meat-eating dinosaur. It walked the floodplains of **North Africa** looking for its prey. This killer may have **hunted large fish** and **sharks** in the water. It might have even been able to **swim**.

Pronounced **SPINE-oh-SORE-us**, its name means thorn lizard.

It was **18 m long** – the length of two buses – and had huge **spines** over its **back**. These spines joined together to form a **sail** about 2 m high. This would have made the beast a frightening **predator**!

Spinosaurus could weigh up to 4,000 kg. That's as much as an **Asian elephant**!

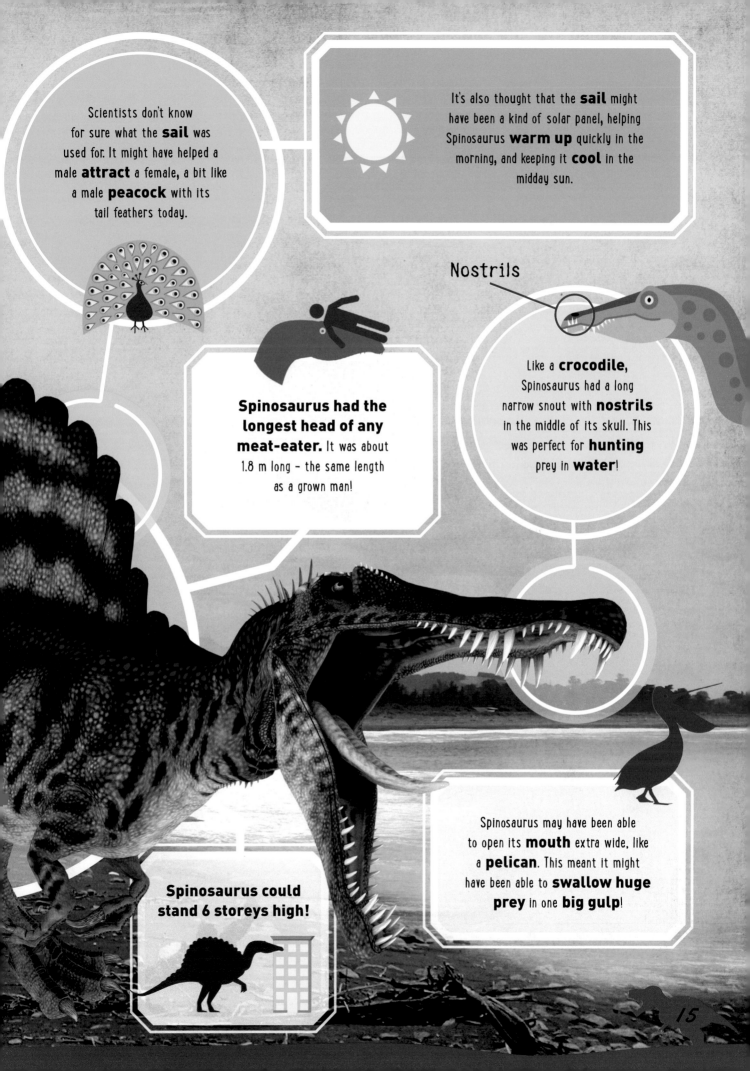

Scientists don't know for sure what the **sail** was used for. It might have helped a male **attract** a female, a bit like a male **peacock** with its tail feathers today.

It's also thought that the **sail** might have been a kind of solar panel, helping Spinosaurus **warm up** quickly in the morning, and keeping it **cool** in the midday sun.

Nostrils

Spinosaurus had the longest head of any meat-eater. It was about 1.8 m long – the same length as a grown man!

Like a **crocodile**, Spinosaurus had a long narrow snout with **nostrils** in the middle of its skull. This was perfect for **hunting** prey in **water**!

Spinosaurus may have been able to open its **mouth** extra wide, like a **pelican**. This meant it might have been able to **swallow huge prey** in one **big gulp**!

Spinosaurus could stand 6 storeys high!

CUTE COELOPHYSIS

In the **Late Triassic** period, a small dinosaur used its **speed** and **agility** to catch tiny reptiles and insects. **Coelophysis** may have only been 3 m long but it was far from cute. This killer had sharp **teeth** and **claws** to hold down and kill its prey.

In 1947, a **fossil** of Coelophysis was found in **New Mexico** at a site called the Ghost Ranch. Since then, hundreds of Coelophysis have been found there. This discovery suggests this meat-eater may have **lived** and **hunted** in **groups**.

New Mexico has made Coelophysis their **state fossil**.

Coelophysis was as **long** as a **small car** and its tail was half its total length!

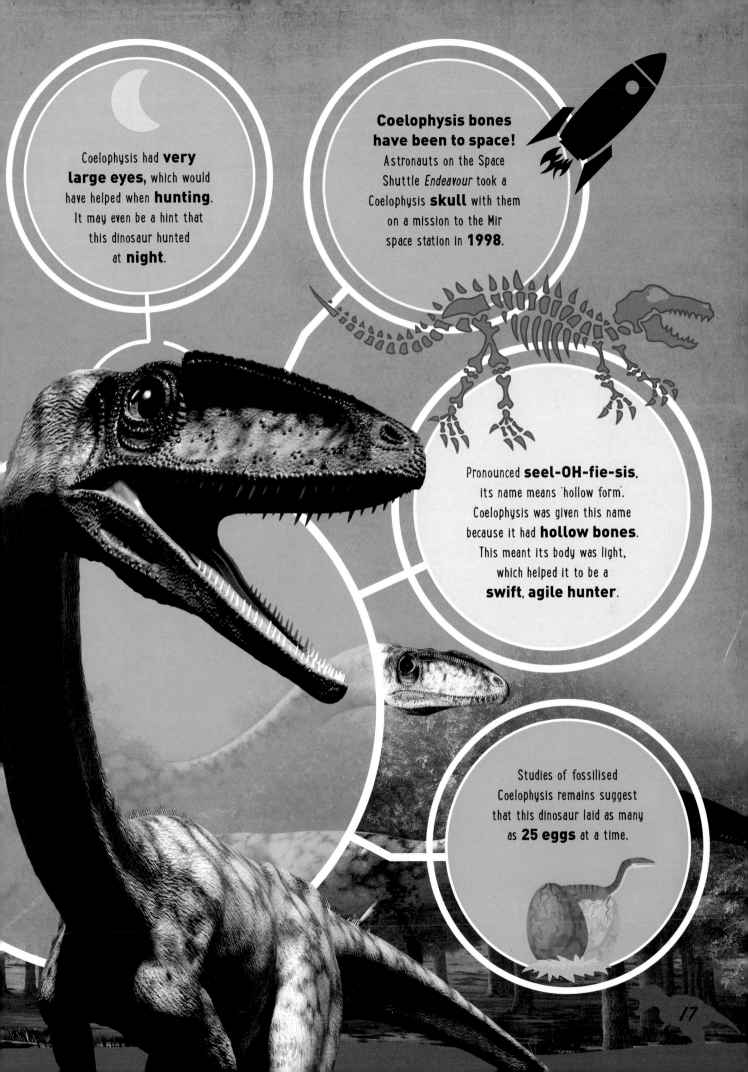

Coelophysis had **very large eyes,** which would have helped when **hunting.** It may even be a hint that this dinosaur hunted at **night.**

Coelophysis bones have been to space! Astronauts on the Space Shuttle *Endeavour* took a Coelophysis **skull** with them on a mission to the Mir space station in **1998.**

Pronounced **seel-OH-fie-sis,** its name means 'hollow form'. Coelophysis was given this name because it had **hollow bones.** This meant its body was light, which helped it to be a **swift, agile hunter.**

Studies of fossilised Coelophysis remains suggest that this dinosaur laid as many as **25 eggs** at a time.

VICIOUS VELOCIRAPTOR

Velociraptor was a small but mighty meat-eater that lived during the Late Cretaceous period, around **84–80 million years ago.**

Pronounced **vel-OSS-ee-rap-tor,** its name means speedy thief.

Velociraptors may have had a fine **feather-like covering** that they used to keep their eggs **warm** when **nesting**.

Velociraptor had strong back **legs** and could run at speeds of up to **65 kilometres per hour!**

With **27–30 teeth** in its **strong jaws**, Velociraptor had just over half the number of teeth as T. rex. It feasted on **prey** such as **reptiles**, **insects** and **smaller dinosaurs**.

It would use its three-fingered **claws** to grab its prey before ripping its flesh with **razor-sharp teeth.**

Velociraptor was about the **size** of a **sheep** and weighed less than a **turkey**.

Its **deadliest** weapon was a huge **9-cm claw** on each of its feet.

GRUESOME GIGANOTOSAURUS

Giganotosaurus means 'giant southern lizard' and this dinosaur was certainly big! It lived during the **Early Cretaceous** period, about 30 million years before the mighty Tyrannosaurus rex walked the Earth!

Pronounced **gig-an-OH-toe-SORE-us**.

Giganotosaurus had a long, narrow tail. It may have helped the dinosaur **turn quickly** when chasing after its prey.

Giganotosaurus could **run** at about **50 kph**. That's as fast as a **car** on a city road.

With its long **chin** and sharp **front teeth**, Giganotosaurus was able to **bite** and **rip** its prey, rather than crushing and crunching it up, like T. rex did.

A Giganotosaurus **brain** was tiny – **the size of a small cucumber**!

Giganotosaurus' **teeth** could grow up to the size of a large **banana**, and had **serrated** edges for slicing through skin and flesh.

This dinosaur could have swallowed a human in one bite!

Each of Giganotosaurus' front **arms** ended in three **fingers**, with three long, curved **claws**, which it used to hold its prey.

This dinosaur could reach up to **12.5 m** in length and weighed **8,000 kg**, which is only a little bit smaller than **two killer whales**. Imagine that running towards you!

GIANT YUTYRANNUS HUALI

In 2012, a giant feathered meat-eater was scientifically named **Yutyrannus huali**. This killer dinosaur was found in China and is the **largest feathered** animal known to have existed.

Yutyrannus was about **9 m long** and weighed **1,300 kg** - about the **weight** of a **small hippo**.

Yutyrannus huali may have used its **feathers** to keep its **nest eggs** warm in the cool habitat it lived in.

Several Yutyrannus hauli **skeletons** have been found in the same location, which could mean this dinosaur **hunted in packs**.

Pronounced **yoo-ti-RAN-us hoo-a-li**, its name is a mix of Mandarin and Latin, and means 'beautiful feathered tyrant'.

Its feathers were up to 20 cm long. The feathers might have helped the dinosaur **blend in** with its habitat of forests and lakes, with cooler winters and possibly snow.

This **Cretaceous** bewast lived during the peak of the dinosaurs' time on Earth. It couldn't fly but its simple **downy covering** probably kept it **warm**.

Before the discovery of Yutyrannus, **Beipiaosaurus** [bay-pyow-sore-us] was the **record holder** for the largest feathered dinosaur. It was **40 times lighter** than Yutyrannus!

2 1 3

FEARSOME FISH-EATERS

Dinosaur **fossil finds** reveal that not all dinosaurs ate meat. Some fancied **fish** for tea!

Suchomimus had over 100 teeth but they weren't very sharp. Its **long snout**, about 2 m in length, was perfect for catching fish.

This toothy beast is a **Suchomimus**, pronounced **sook-oh-mim-us**. Its name means crocodile mimic.

Suchomimus was a dinosaur that may have dined on **fish** as well as meat. It roamed the river banks of **Early Cretaceous period Africa** looking for prey.

Scientists wonder if Suchomimus may have **swam** and **dived** for food, too.

Suchomimus was huge! It was 11m long and 3 m tall. It weighed 2,700 kg.

Suchomimus would have needed **large prey** to satisfy its appetite. It probably feasted on **Mawsonia** [Mor-SO-nee-ah], a big prehistoric fish that could grow up to 4 m long. That's about the same size as a rhinoceros!

Baryonyx's **claw** on its thumb was **30 cm long** – that's as long as this book. It may have used the large claw to **spear fish**.

This scary creature is a **Baryonyx**, pronounced **bah-ree-ON-icks**. Its name means heavy claw.

Baryonyx was a fish-eating dinosaur that lived during the Early Cretaceous period. Its **crocodile-like jaws** were perfect for snatching fish from the water.

Fish-eating dinosaurs used their **long jaws** and **strong necks** to grab their prey out of the water with powerful, darting strikes.

Palaeontologists know that Baryonyx was a **fish-eater** because **fish scales** have been found in the stomach region of some **fossil** discoveries.

Baryonyx's **jagged teeth** curved inwards to make it hard for a fish to escape!

25

BURIED BONES

Palaeontologists use fossil finds to learn about mighty meat-eating dinosaurs of the past. The fossil pieces fit together like a jigsaw puzzle to reveal what the dinosaur looked like and how it lived.

Tyrannosaurus rex had around 200 bones in its body.

T. rex fought one another.
One famous T. rex fossil, Sue, had **bite** marks on her face from another T. rex!

Fossilised dinosaur poo, called **coprolite**, was found in Canada. It probably came from a T. rex and was the size of a sandwich. The coprolite contained bones from another dinosaur – maybe a young **Triceratops**.

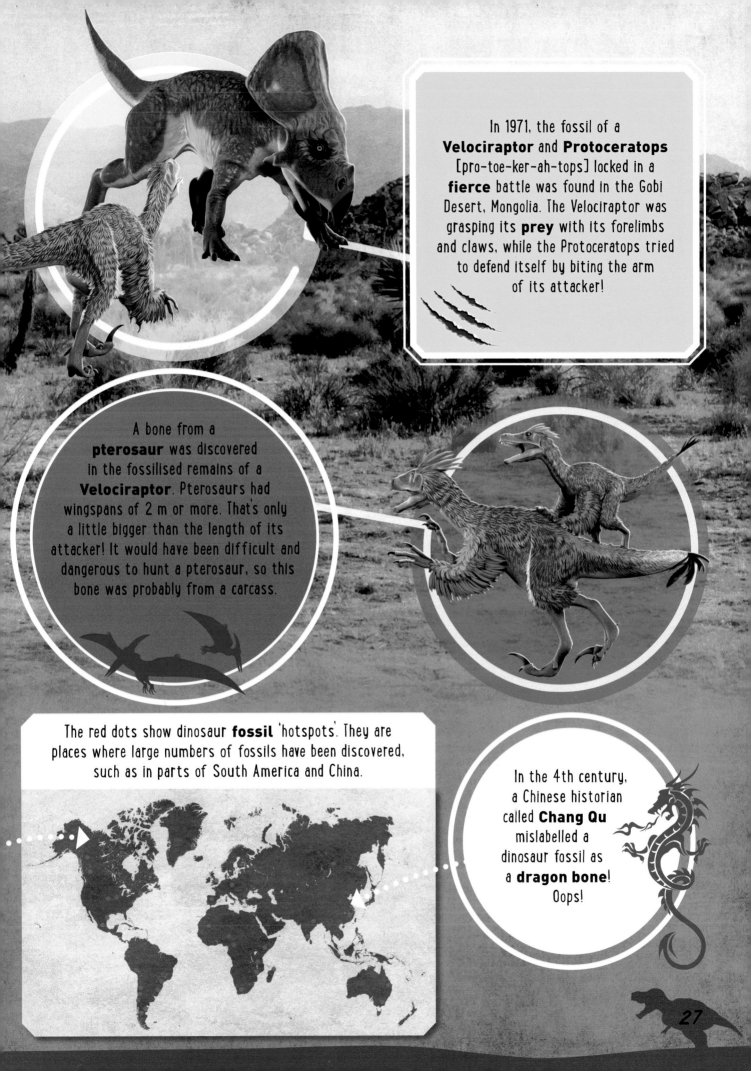

In 1971, the fossil of a **Velociraptor** and **Protoceratops** [pro-toe-ker-ah-tops] locked in a **fierce** battle was found in the Gobi Desert, Mongolia. The Velociraptor was grasping its **prey** with its forelimbs and claws, while the Protoceratops tried to defend itself by biting the arm of its attacker!

A bone from a **pterosaur** was discovered in the fossilised remains of a **Velociraptor**. Pterosaurs had wingspans of 2 m or more. That's only a little bigger than the length of its attacker! It would have been difficult and dangerous to hunt a pterosaur, so this bone was probably from a carcass.

The red dots show dinosaur **fossil** 'hotspots'. They are places where large numbers of fossils have been discovered, such as in parts of South America and China.

In the 4th century, a Chinese historian called **Chang Qu** mislabelled a dinosaur fossil as a **dragon bone**! Oops!

27

MORE DINO FACTS

Meat-eating dinosaurs were some of the fiercest creatures to ever walk the Earth. Check out these fun dino facts!

ALLOSAURUS

HEIGHT: 3 m
LENGTH: 12 m
WEIGHT: 2,100 kg
LIVED: Late Jurassic
LOCATION: Portugal, USA
FIRST FOSSIL DISCOVERY: Colorado, USA, 1869
FACT: Allosaurus poo has been found measuring 1.5 m - about the size of a car!

COELOPHYSIS

HEIGHT: 1.8 m
LENGTH: 3 m
WEIGHT: 27 kg
LIVED: Late Jurassic
LOCATION: USA
FIRST FOSSIL DISCOVERY: New Mexico, USA, 1881
FACT: It is thought that Coelophysis bit their prey like Komodo dragons do today.

UTAHRAPTOR

HEIGHT: 1.7 m
LENGTH: 6 m
WEIGHT: 1,000 kg
LIVED: Early Cretaceous
LOCATION: USA
FIRST FOSSIL DISCOVERY: Utah, USA, 1975
FACT: Utahraptor is the largest raptor discovered to date.

SPINOSAURUS

HEIGHT: 7 m
LENGTH: 18 m
WEIGHT: up to 20,000 kg
LIVED: Late Cretaceous
LOCATION: Egypt, Morocco
FIRST FOSSIL DISCOVERY: Egypt, 1912
FACT: Spinosaurus may have sometimes walked on all fours.

MICRORAPTOR

HEIGHT: 0.3 m
LENGTH: 0.8 m
WEIGHT: 1-2 kg
LIVED: Early Cretaceous
LOCATION: China
FIRST FOSSIL DISCOVERY: Liaoning, China, 2000
FACT: This meat-eater ate birds, so it might have spent some of its life high up in trees.

DEINONYCHUS

HEIGHT: 0.9 m
LENGTH: 3 m
WEIGHT: 75 kg
LIVED: Early Cretaceous
LOCATION: USA
FIRST FOSSIL DISCOVERY: Montana, USA, 1931
FACT: Deinonychus had the same bite force as an alligator.

GLOSSARY

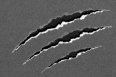

agile to move quickly and easily

balance to stay upright and steady

carcass the dead body of an animal

carnivore an animal that eats meat

coprolite scientific term for fossilised poo

Cretaceous period a period in Earth's history, between 144 and 65 million years ago

downy covered with fine, soft hair or feathers

extinct when a type of animal dies out completely

flood plain an area of low-lying ground next to a river or stream

food chain a group of living things (animals and plants) where each member of the group is eaten in turn by another

fossil the remains of an animal or plant, preserved for millions of years

habitat the place where an animal or a plant lives

hunt to pursue and kill other animals for food

Jurassic period a period of Earth's history, between 206 and 144 million years ago

nocturnal to be active at night and sleep during the day

pack a group of wild animals

paleontologist a scientist who studies fossils

predator an animal that eats other animals

prey an animal that is eaten by other animals

pterosaur giant flying reptile

scavenger an animal that feeds on dead plants or animals

stalk to pursue another animal, usually while hunting

state fossil the fossil of one species chosen by an American state

storey the part of a building where all rooms are on the same level

talon a claw

theropods a group of meat-eating dinosaurs

Triassic period a period in Earth's history, between 248 and 206 million years ago

FURTHER INFORMATION

Further Reading

Professor Pete's Prehistoric Animals: Giant Meat-Eating Dinosaurs by David West (Franklin Watts, 2017)

Prehistoric Safari: Killer Dinosaurs by Liz Miles (Franklin Watts, 2013)

Planet Earth: Birth of the Dinosaurs by Michael Bright (Wayland, 2016)

Would you Rather… Have the Teeth of a T Rex or the Armour of an Ankylosaurus? by Mel Howells and Camilla de le Bédoyère (QED Publishing, 2016)

Websites

www.natgeokids.com/uk/discover/animals/prehistoric-animals/steve_brusatte/

www.bbc.co.uk/nature/17159086

www.nhm.ac.uk/discover/dino-directory/index.html

INDEX

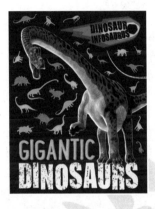